A TRUE BOOK™

The Most Endangered
Rhinos

KATIE MARSICO

Children's Press®
An Imprint of Scholastic Inc.

Content Consultant
Dr. Stephen S. Ditchkoff
Professor of Wildlife Sciences
Auburn University, Auburn, Alabama

Library of Congress Cataloging-in-Publication Data
Names: Marsico, Katie, 1980– author.
Title: Rhinos / by Katie Marsico.
Other titles: True book.
Description: New York : Children's Press, [2017] | Series: A true book
Identifiers: LCCN 2016025108| ISBN 9780531227299 (library binding) | ISBN 9780531232804 (pbk.)
Subjects: LCSH: Rhinoceroses—Juvenile literature. | Rhinoceroses—Conservation—Juvenile
  literature.
Classification: LCC QL737.U63 M345 2017 | DDC 599.66/8—dc23
LC record available at https://lccn.loc.gov/2016025108

© 2017 Scholastic Inc.
All rights reserved. Published in 2017 by Children's Press, an imprint of Scholastic Inc.
Printed in China 62

SCHOLASTIC, CHILDREN'S PRESS, A TRUE BOOK™, and associated logos are trademarks and/or
registered trademarks of Scholastic Inc.
1 2 3 4 5 6 7 8 9 10 R 26 25 24 23 22 21 20 19 18 17

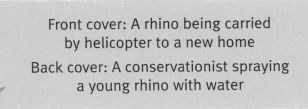

Front cover: A rhino being carried
by helicopter to a new home
Back cover: A conservationist spraying
a young rhino with water

Find the Truth!

Everything you are about to read is true *except* for one of the sentences on this page.

Which one is **TRUE**?

T or F Rhino horns contain ivory.

T or F Only about 60 Javan rhinos exist in the wild.

Find the answers in this book.

Contents

THE **BIG** TRUTH!

Raising Orphaned Rhinos

Mother rhino and baby

Male rhinos fighting during mating season

3 The Risks That Rhinos Face

What specific situations challenge
rhinos' survival? 27

4 A Chance to Change the Story

How do various conservation
efforts help protect rhinos? 35

A baby rhino
follows a park
ranger

A baby rhino runs through Kariega Game Reserve.

CHAPTER 1

Fighting for a Future

The Kariega Game Reserve stretches across 39 square miles (101 square kilometers) of majestic South African wilderness. The area is teeming with wildlife, including two species of rhinoceros. Visitors from around the world travel to Kariega to catch a glimpse of these remarkable mammals. Yet the reserve sometimes attracts more than just tourists. On March 2, 2012, **poachers** attacked three of Kariega's rhinos.

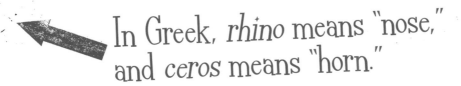

In Greek, *rhino* means "nose," and *ceros* means "horn."

Dr. William Fowlds tries to restrain a rhino to perform a procedure.

Rhino Rescue

The poachers cut off the rhinos' horns, leaving the animals with serious facial injuries. In certain cultures, rhino horns are used to make everything from dagger handles to traditional medicines.

Wildlife veterinarian Dr. William Fowlds attempted to save the injured rhinos. Only one survived. Her caretakers named her Thandi. Dr. Fowlds and his team nursed Thandi back to health and performed surgery to reconstruct her face.

Thandi slowly recovered. In December 2013, Dr. Fowlds was overjoyed to discover Thandi was pregnant! The rhino gave birth to a healthy calf named Thembi on January 13, 2015. In the Xhosa language, which is spoken throughout South Africa, *thembi* means "hope."

Rhinos like Thandi face many threats, but **conservationists** are working to help these animals survive.

Thandi is a white rhino.

How Many Horns?

Rhinos are large, hooved mammals that are related to horses, donkeys, tapirs, and zebras. Depending on the species, rhinos have one or two horns on their nose. The black rhinos and white rhinos in Africa have two horns. So do Sumatran rhinos, which live in Asia. The other two Asian species—Indian and Javan rhinos—have only one horn.

Where Rhinos Live

A Javan rhino takes a swim in a river in Indonesia.

Rhino Alert

Black, Javan, and Sumatran rhinos are critically endangered. This means that they're at an extremely high risk of **extinction**. Indian rhinos are considered vulnerable, which means the risk is not as severe but remains high. Scientists believe that white rhinos have the most stable population. Even this species, however, is near threatened. In other words, it is likely that white rhinos will eventually experience the threat of extinction.

An earthquake and tsunami destroyed this Indonesian beach and overturned a nearby ship in 2005.

Poaching has caused rhinos to rank among Earth's most endangered creatures. **Habitat** loss, natural disasters, and disease have also reduced their numbers. A lack of **genetic** diversity, or variety, has affected certain species, too.

Despite such challenges, conservationists are determined to protect rhinos. They understand that the survival of these animals impacts both wildlife and people.

Role Reversal

People sometimes become rhino poachers out of desperation. In certain areas, poverty and political conflict make it difficult to find good-paying jobs. When given the chance, however, such individuals often prove their desire to change. These former poachers eventually abandon illegal hunting to work as wildlife trackers and photographers. They use their nature skills and knowledge of rhino habitats to support conservation.

A rhino grazes on grass in the Maasai Mara National Reserve in Kenya.

Incredible Animals

Rhinos exist in several different types of habitats throughout Asia and Africa. Some live in **scrublands** and grasslands. Others are found in tropical forests and deserts. Because rhinos are herbivores, they primarily feed on plant life. A rhino's diet is usually made up of grasses and the leaves of various trees and bushes.

Some rhinos eat up to 220 species of plants.

Almost the Largest Land Mammals

Rhinos are some of Earth's largest land mammals. In terms of size, they're second only to elephants.

A COMPARISON OF RHINO SPECIES				
Species	**Weight (Adults)**	**Geographic Range**	**Habitat**	**Feeding Habits and Diet**
Black rhino	1,760 to 3,080 pounds (798 to 1,397 kilograms)	Namibia and coastal East Africa	Deserts and grasslands	Browsers, feeding on high-growing plant matter; eat fruit and leaves from bushes and trees
Indian rhino	4,000 to 6,000 pounds (1,814 to 2,722 kg)	Eastern Himalayas	Forests and grasslands	Primarily grazers, feeding on low-growing plant matter; eat grasses and leaves and fruit found on shrubs and other low plants
Javan rhino	1,984 to 5,071 pounds (900 to 2,300 kg)	Java, Indonesia	Forests	Both browsers and grazers; eat shoots, twigs, and fallen fruit
Sumatran rhino	1,320 to 2,090 pounds (599 to 948 kg)	Borneo and Sumatra	Forests	Browsers, feeding on fruit, leaves, twigs, and bark
White rhino	3,080 to 7,920 pounds (1,397 to 3,592 kg)	Namibia and coastal East Africa	Grasslands	Grazers, feeding on grasses

Rhinos have three toes on each foot.

Built for Survival

All five species of rhino share certain features. Their skin, which is usually gray or brown, is up to 1.8 inches (45.7 millimeters) thick! This protects them from sharp grasses and thorns.

Underneath a rhino's skin are powerful muscles. Rhinos use these muscles to raise and lower their large head, as well as to walk and run. Some rhinos reach speeds of 30 miles (48.3 km) per hour!

Which Senses Are Strongest?

Rhinos have poor eyesight. But their other senses make up for it. Their cup-shaped ears rotate, which helps them hear noises from all directions. In addition, their large nose can sniff out animals up to 0.25 mile (0.4 km) away. That's the length of about three and a half football fields.

These super senses help alert rhinos to the presence of **predators**. Big cats and crocodiles occasionally hunt younger rhinos. So do hyenas and wild dogs.

Young rhinos and their mothers must be on the lookout for crocodiles and other potential predators.

An Indian rhino shows its sharp front teeth as it chews.

Types of Teeth

There are a few different ways rhinos defend themselves in the wild. One involves their teeth. Depending on the species, rhinos have between 24 and 34 teeth. Most of the time, the teeth just tear and grind up plant matter. In the case of Indian rhinos, however, certain teeth are longer and more pointed. When charging at enemies, Indian rhinos use these teeth as slashing weapons.

A black rhino mother nuzzles her calf with her horn.

Horns at Work

Sometimes rhinos depend on their horns for self-defense. These hard, pointed body parts are capable of ripping into the flesh of potential predators. Rhinos battle each other with their horns as well. They fight over **territory** or access to certain **mates**. Mother rhinos also use their horns to gently nudge their babies along. Horns even serve as shovels to uncover plants and dig for water sources.

A Look at the Life Cycle

Rhinos are usually ready to reproduce when they are between six and eight years of age. Female rhinos, or cows, are pregnant for 15 to 16 months! Normally, they give birth to only one calf at a time.

Babies are born without a horn. At first, they're completely dependent on cows for both food and protection. Calves remain with their mothers for two to three years.

Calves stay close by their mother until they are old enough to take care of themselves.

Two white rhino males fight during mating season.

Rhino Life

In the wild, rhinos live 35 to 40 years. During that time, they generally prefer to be solitary, or alone. Occasionally, species such as white rhinos and Indian rhinos are found in small groups. For the most part, however, rhinos only come together to **reproduce**. They may also fight when they meet. Males, or bulls, are highly territorial. This means they fiercely protect the area where they live. Females are extremely protective of their young.

Rhino Talk

Communication among rhinos takes many different forms. These include a variety of noises such as growls, grunts, bellows, and snorts. Sometimes rhinos also send signals through body language. For example, when they lower their horns to the ground, they're often warning other animals to stay away. For rhinos, even waste, or dung, provides an opportunity to communicate. Unique scents within the dung help rhinos mark their territory.

Snort! Grunt!

Grunts, snorts, and other sounds help a rhino share its feelings.

Raising Orphaned Rhinos

Many calves have lost their parents to poaching. Orphaned calves rarely survive on their own. Luckily, organizations such as South Africa's Rhino Orphanage help raise orphaned baby rhinos. The organization's goal is to eventually return its residents to the wild.

**BOTTLE-FED
A SPECIAL FORMULA**
Volunteers give calves at the orphanage bottles every three hours. During feedings, babies drink 0.5 gallons (2 liters) of special milk. Caretakers must weigh and blend ingredients to create a formula similar to rhino's milk.

STARTING SOLID FOODS

In the wild, mother rhinos help their babies gradually switch from milk to plants. At the orphanage, caretakers sometimes whip up grass smoothies in a blender to help youngsters adjust to solid food. Staff members may even drop to their hands and knees to "show" calves how to graze.

BEDTIME FOR BABY

Babies that have just lost their mothers need a lot of reassurance. They might also be injured or ill. Caretakers often sleep alongside the rhinos to monitor them overnight. These volunteers are accustomed to restless rhinos kicking them during the night.

WARM UP, COOL DOWN!

The rhinos need exercise every day, so volunteers take them for walks. Of course, rhinos also need to cool down. In the wild, they watch their mothers beat the heat with a mud bath. Staff members at the orphanage frequently have to demonstrate this behavior.

CHAPTER 3

The Risks That Rhinos Face

The future of rhinos is important for many reasons. These animals impact the overall health of the **ecosystems** where they live. Because rhinos eat plants, their dung contains seeds. When they produce waste, the seeds in their droppings later grow into plants that become food for other animals. Rhinos also support humans. People hoping to see them in the wild fuel the tourism industry in parts of Africa and Asia.

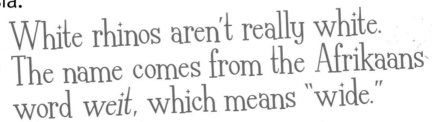

White rhinos aren't really white. The name comes from the Afrikaans word *weit*, which means "wide."

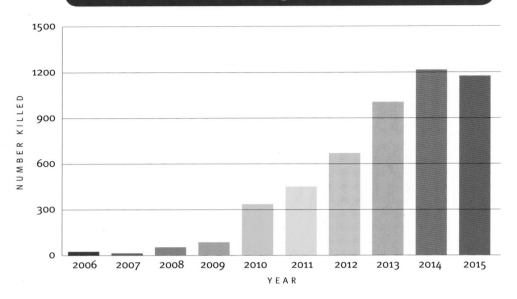

Recorded Rhino Poaching Deaths in South Africa

Hunting for Horns

Poaching is a major threat to rhinos. Their horns contain the protein keratin, which is the same substance found in human nails. It's a common substance, but some people believe powder made from rhino horns has special qualities. In some parts of the world, it's a prized ingredient in traditional medicines. Such medicines are used to treat everything from fever to blood disorders to cancer.

Traditional medicines are not all that drives rhino poaching. Throughout the Middle East, rhino horns are carved into the curved handles of daggers called jambiyas. Such knives are seen as a sign of wealth and social status. In other situations, illegal trophy hunters slaughter rhinos for sport. Such hunters view the killing of these massive mammals as evidence of their skills.

Jambiyas feature detailed carvings. They typically are expensive.

Shrinking Habitat

Habitat loss has also taken a severe toll on rhino populations. In Sumatra, for example, people clear forests to make space for rice and coffee farms. This destruction of natural spaces limits where Sumatran rhinos are able to feed and reproduce. Land development and the logging industry in parts of Asia and Africa have a similar effect on other rhino species. Local wars increase human traffic in wild ecosystems, disturbing rhinos and other wildlife.

Rice farmers sometimes grow their crops in areas that also serve as rhino habitats.

Up in the Air

Sometimes rhinos need help relocating to habitats with plenty to eat and more potential mates. How do conservationists move mammals that weigh thousands of pounds? By helicopter! Many veterinarians believe this is the safest method. Beforehand, the animals receive a medicine that makes them sleep. During the flight, rhinos typically hang upside down from the helicopters. At the end of the flight, the pilot carefully lowers its cargo into land vehicles. Then the rhinos are driven to their final destination.

Cattle sometimes carry diseases that can infect local wildlife.

Disease and Natural Disasters

Diseases such as tuberculosis also threaten rhino populations. Tuberculosis is a disease that affects many species, including humans. The illness mainly affects the lungs. Cattle, owned by ranchers, frequently bring this and other sicknesses into an environment. Local wild animals catch the illnesses and often die. Those who become sick also help spread the disease farther into wild populations.

Natural disasters such as tsunamis and volcanic eruptions threaten rhinos, too. Such disasters have the potential to wipe out what remains of critically endangered species. Javan rhinos in particular are in danger. Parts of the population live in an area of Indonesia that is close to the ocean. A nearby volcanic eruption could trigger a tsunami, which could kill all the rhinos there at once.

Tsunamis have a history of causing vast destruction in Indonesia and surrounding areas.

Some rhinos are under the protection of rangers.

A Chance to Change the Story

Rhino conservation involves far more than recognizing a series of problems. It's also about finding solutions. This includes strengthening efforts to end poaching and the illegal horn trade.

Conservationists use electronic transmitters, drones, and camera traps to monitor wild rhino populations. Camera traps are equipped with motion and light sensors. They allow scientists to obtain photographs and video footage of rhinos while working in another location.

Saving a Species

By observing wild rhinos, conservationists learn more about the animals and the threats they face. Conservationists also team up with authorities to patrol locations that are hot spots in the illegal wildlife trade. These include wilderness areas, borders, and ports. In addition, conservationists encourage government officials to enforce restrictions on rhino hunting. If someone violates conservation laws, it's important that they're held accountable for their actions.

A Troubling Rhino Timeline

8,000 years ago
A species known as woolly rhinos becomes extinct.

1960
An estimated 2,000 northern white rhinos, a subspecies of white rhino, remain.

50 million years ago
The earliest rhinos appear.

Habitat Help

Other efforts focus on protecting and restoring natural habitats. This means reaching out to park officials and local communities to stop **deforestation**. It also includes replanting trees, bushes, and grasses that serve as rhino food sources.

Sometimes conservationists relocate rhino populations to new habitats. Such moves increase genetic diversity. They also lessen the odds that any single disaster or event will completely wipe out a species.

1970
Total rhino populations are down 90 percent from historic times.

2011
A subspecies of Javan rhino becomes extinct in Vietnam.

2015
Only three northern white rhinos remain on Earth.

Raising Populations and Awareness

How long each rhino species will survive without help is anyone's guess. Scientists believe that there are 20,170 white rhinos in the wild. That number is likely more than 5,000 for black rhinos and more than 3,000 for Indian rhinos. Conservationists estimate between 220 and 275 Sumatran rhinos exist in their natural habitats. That number is only about 60 for Javan rhinos!

Rhino Species Populations

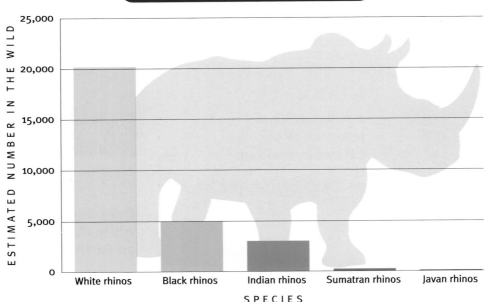

A young rhino chases after a ball at a zoo in New Mexico. Toys help zoo animals stay entertained and active.

Conservationists try to use captive breeding programs to further boost rhino populations. These programs typically occur in zoos and research centers. The idea is to eventually release rhinos born in captivity into the wild.

In the meantime, conservationists continue to educate the public. They share information on why rhinos desperately need people's protection. By increasing awareness about these amazing mammals, they also increase hope of their survival. ★

CALLING ALL CONSERVATIONISTS!

Conservationists represent all walks of life. Some are scientists. Others are kids just like you! What can you do to help? Here are a few ideas to get you started.

GET THE WORD OUT

World Rhino Day is September 22. Work with your teachers and student council. Ask if you can hang posters and notecards with rhino facts around school. Also try to arrange guest speakers. Local zoos and conservation groups are great places to start. Call or e-mail to find out if these organizations have employees or volunteers who are rhino experts.

"ADOPT" A RHINO

Organize a bake sale or community car wash. Use the money you earn to sponsor a rhino. With the help of an adult, check out the Web sites of zoos and organizations. Learn about their adoption programs. Don't worry, you won't end up with a massive mammal on your doorstep! Instead, you'll probably receive photos and updates about your rhino.

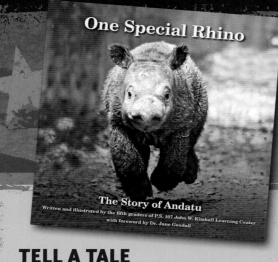

One Special Rhino

The Story of Andatu

Written and illustrated by the fifth graders of P.S. 107 John W. Kimball Learning Center with foreword by Dr. Jane Goodall

TELL A TALE

Recently, fifth graders in Brooklyn, New York, wrote and illustrated *One Special Rhino: The Story of Andatu*. Their efforts turned into a published book. Perhaps yours will, too! Write a short story or poem. Maybe imagine life as an endangered animal. Or pretend you're a conservationist working to save rhinos. Be creative! When you finish, share what you wrote.

START A CLUB

Start your own conservation club! It doesn't have to be huge. It could be just you and a few friends. Meet every week to talk about the latest events involving rhino conservation. Don't forget to discuss how *you* can help protect rhinos and other animals!

International Horn Trade

Buying and selling rhino horns has been illegal for many years. However, that is changing. In May 2016, the South African government legalized the rhino horn trade in the country. Nevertheless, rhino horns still cannot be traded in other countries. People both for and against legalizing the international horn trade argue that they're helping rhinos.

Which side do you agree with? Why?

Yes Lift bans on the international horn trade!

The best way to end rhino poaching is to regulate, or control, the horn trade. **Making it illegal won't erase the demand for rhino horns.** Buyers will simply purchase the horns from illegal sources, such as poachers. Furthermore, some South African ranchers legally raise rhinos. Occasionally, they safely remove the rhinos' horns, which eventually grow back. **These ranchers have built up huge stores of rhino horns**. One rancher has even collected 5 tons. It's impossible for them to legally sell their goods in other countries.

Besides, if ranchers flood the market with stockpiles of horns, **the supply of horns will increase. As a result, the demand will decrease and prices will drop**. Ultimately, poachers will be out of business!

No Do not lift bans on the international horn trade!

Poachers will still find ways to profit from illegal hunting. Also, is it possible to know for sure how the demand for rhino horns will change? For instance, if traditional medicines become more popular, the demand for rhino horns might go up, not down.

Lifting international bans would send a dangerous message. Officials would be supporting the trade of products made from animals threatened by extinction. What might this mean for other species?

Most rhino populations aren't stable, making it too risky to experiment with legal changes. The short-term effects of lifting international bans only benefit certain groups of people. The long-term effects could bring rhinos closer to extinction!

True Statistics

The number of rhino species: 5

The number of rhino species that are critically endangered: 3

The weight range of most rhinos: 1,320 to 7,920 lbs. (599 to 3,592 kg)

The maximum thickness of rhino skin: 1.8 in. (45.7 mm)

The speed some rhinos reach: 30 mph (48.3 kph)

The number of teeth rhinos have: Between 24 and 34

The life span of rhinos in the wild: 35 to 40 years

The number of months rhinos are pregnant: 15 to 16

The amount of time rhino calves remain with their mother: 2 to 3 years

The number of Javan rhinos that exist in their natural habitats: Around 60

Did you find the truth?

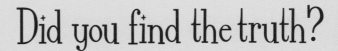

F Rhino horns contain ivory.

T Only about 60 Javan rhinos exist in the wild.

Resources

Books

Claus, Matteson. *Animals and Deforestation*. New York: Gareth Stevens Publishing, 2014.

Meeker, Clare Hodgson. *Rhino Rescue! And More True Stories of Saving Animals*. Washington, DC: National Geographic, 2016.

Shea, Nicole. *Poaching and Illegal Trade*. New York: Gareth Stevens Publishing, 2014.

Visit this Scholastic Web site for more information about rhinos and to download the Teaching Guide for this series:

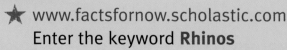 www.factsfornow.scholastic.com
Enter the keyword **Rhinos**

Important Words

conservationists (kahn-sur-VAY-shuhn-ists) people who work to protect valuable things, especially forests, wildlife, natural resources, or artistic or historic objects

deforestation (dee-for-is-TAY-shuhn) the removal or cutting down of forests

ecosystems (EE-koh-sis-tuhmz) all the living things in a particular area

extinction (ik-STINGKT-shuhn) the permanent disappearance of a living thing

genetic (juh-NET-ik) passed from one generation to the next

habitat (HAB-uh-tat) the place where an animal or plant is usually found

mates (MAYTS) animals that join together to reproduce

poachers (POH-churz) people who hunt or fish illegally

predators (PREH-duh-turz) animals that live by hunting other animals for food

reproduce (ree-pruh-DOOS) to produce offspring

scrublands (SKRUHB-landz) areas that are covered with small bushes and trees

territory (TER-uh-tor-ee) a claimed area of land

Index

Page numbers in **bold** indicate illustrations.

About the Author

Katie Marsico graduated from Northwestern University and worked as an editor in reference publishing before she began writing in 2006. Since that time, she has published more than 200 titles for children and young adults. Rhinos are among Ms. Marsico's favorite animals!